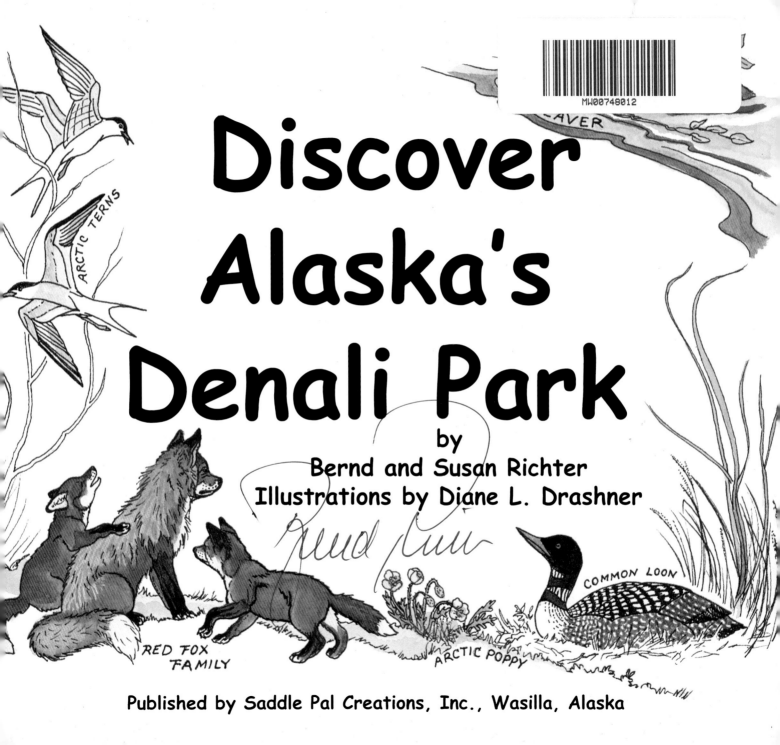

Discover Alaska's Denali Park

by
Bernd and Susan Richter
Illustrations by Diane L. Drashner

Published by Saddle Pal Creations, Inc., Wasilla, Alaska

Acknowledgements:
Thanks to Linda Thurston and Jan O'Meara for editorial comments and suggestions.
Thanks to family and friends for moral support.

Dedicated to the effort of those who make sure that
Denali National Park and Preserve remains the special place it is.

More children's books by Bernd and Susan Richter available
from Saddle Pal Creations, Inc.:

* When Grandma and Grandpa Visited Alaska They ...
* Grandma and Grandpa Cruise Alaska's Inside Passage
* Grandma and Grandpa Visit Denali National Park
* Grandma and Grandpa Ride the Alaska Train
* Alaska Animals - Where Do They Go at 40 Below?
* Touch and Feel Alaska's Animals (board book)
* Uncover Alaska's Wonders (a lift-the-flap book)
* The Little Bear Who Didn't Want to Hibernate
* Traveling Alaska
* Goodnight Alaska - Goodnight Little Bear (board book)
* Peek-A-Boo Alaska (lift-the-flap board book)
* How Animal Moms Love Their Babies (board book)
* When Grandma and Grandpa cruised through AK (board book)

* How Alaska Got Its Flag (with flag song CD)
* The Twelve Days of Christmas in Alaska
* Do Alaskans Live in Igloos?
* Cruising Alaska's Inside Passage
* Listen to Alaska's Animals (sound book)
* She's My Mommy Too!
* When Grandma visited Alaska she ...
* Alaskan Toys for Girls and Boys
* My Alaska Animals - Can You Name Them?
* A Bus Ride Into Denali (board book)
* Grandma and Grandpa Love Their RV
* Old Maid - Alaska Style (card game)
.... and more

Look at these books by visiting our website **www.alaskachildrensbooks.com**

Dear ....,

National parks are great places to visit because there is so much to see and to do. Denali National Park in Alaska has the highest mountains and the most amazing animals of any park in North America. Being at that park and seeing all its wonderful scenery and wildlife is a trip of a lifetime you are invited to take with this beautiful picture book.

Enjoy this discovery tour through magnificent Denali National Park and Preserve.

Love, ...

As you can see on the map, Alaska is by far the largest of the 50 states that form the United States of America. Even so, only about 650,000 people live there. This leaves vast areas of land that are relatively undisturbed by human impact. This is a perfect setting for wildlife to exist. To ensure that wildlife will continue to thrive as nature intended and to preserve beautiful areas for future generations to enjoy, the U.S. Congress created many national parks during the past 100 years, including Denali National Park and Preserve.

Can you name any national parks?
Have you ever been to one?

Fairbanks

Denali
National Park
and Preserve

Anchorage

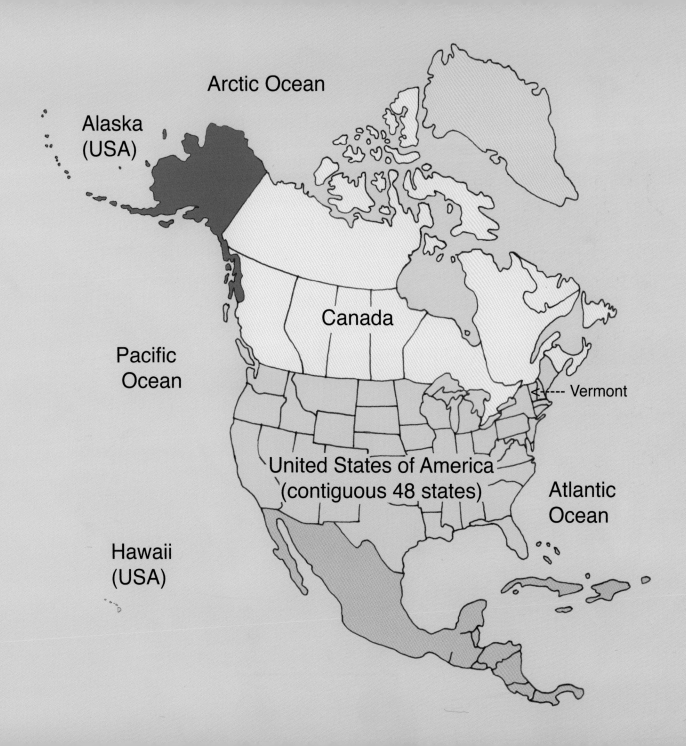

TALL FIREWEED

PHOEBUS PARNASSIAN

At 6 million acres, Denali National Park and Preserve is as big as the state of Vermont. Considering this, it is surprising to learn that there is only a single gravel road that leads into and out of the park. One road - the rest of the park is almost untouched wilderness for animals to live in freely. To protect animals from traffic on that road, most visitors see the park by bus. That's what we will be doing together now.

Bus trips start at the Wilderness Access Center or at nearby hotels. Let's meet the driver who will also be our guide on this trip.

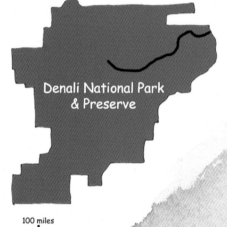

Denali National Park & Preserve

0   100 miles

0   100 km

Wow, we've gone down the road only a few miles and here's our first magnificent animal sighting. It's a bull moose, as you can tell by the big antlers.

"This one probably weighs around 1,400 pounds," the driver says. He also mentions that it is common to see moose in this tree-covered area of the park. "Moose like it here because the trees provide protection from predators, such as wolf and bear, which live here as well."

This tree-covered area is called "boreal forest" or "taiga." Moose call it "breakfast, lunch, and dinner." Can you see what other animals are hiding out in this forest?

"Keep your eyes out for snowshoe hare, fox, wolverine, and lynx, as well as eagles and hawks," the driver urges. Which of those can you find in this picture?

SINGING VOLE

LYNX

SHED ANTLER GNAWED BY RODENTS

ED SQUIRREL   MASKED SHREW   SNOWSHOE HARE   SPRUCE GROUSE (MALE)

Oh look, birds, right next to the road!

"These are ptarmigan," the driver says. "They are Alaska's state bird and they are real masters of camouflage. In the summer, their earth-brown plumage blends in perfectly with the vegetation they hide in and feed on. In the winter, they grow a white plumage that blends in perfectly with the snow. This way, they are camouflaged from their predators the entire year. Other animals that turn white in the winter include the arctic fox, the ermine, and the snowshoe hare. Some of them, of course, are predators themselves."

PTARMIGAN AND SNOWSHOE HARE IN WINTER WHITE

What's this? Is this already the end of the trip?

"No, no, not to worry," the driver explains. "Up to this point, the first 14 miles, the road is open for everybody. But from here on and for the next 76 miles, either a special permit or a bus ticket is required to continue farther into the park. Traffic is restricted to protect the park and its animals."

This friendly park ranger welcomes the visitors to Denali National Park and Preserve. She checks the permit and then explains some of the park rules, which are: don't bring into the park what you can't take out; don't take out what you didn't bring in; don't get too close to animals because they are wild and possibly dangerous; don't feed the animals because this isn't a zoo; and don't make loud noises that could disturb the animals.

Wow! Look at these beautiful flowers! This must be Primrose Ridge.

Just as the animals, plants are protected in the park. Even non-living things, such as rocks and water, are protected, because together with all living matter they form one large system called an "ecosystem." For example, it's the soil and the water that help plants to grow. The plants, in turn, keep the soil from being washed away by running water. Some animals, like the bees, help the flowers by spreading pollen. Other animals, however, like this cute arctic ground squirrel, may come along and eat the flowers. But watch out little squirrel, somebody may try to catch you!

ALPINE ARNICA

FRIGID ARNICA

MOSS CAMPION

LOW-BUSH CRANBERRY

LABRADOR TEA

PINK PLUME

FRIGID SHOOTING STAR

MOUNTAIN HAREBELL

ARCTIC LUPINE

ALPINE FORGET-ME-NOT

ARCTIC POPPY

DWARF FIREWEED   TUNDRA ROSE   BLUEBELLS   TALL FIREWEED
BERIAN ASTER   MOUNTAIN AVENS   WILD GERANIUM

"Caribou at 10 o'clock," somebody on the bus yells out. Do you know what that means? Well, luckily, the driver had explained before that everybody should imagine the bus as a clock, with the front of the bus as 12 o'clock and the back as 6 o'clock. So now all look toward the left and forward, where 10 would be on a 'bus clock.' If you'd like to, we can play 'bus clock' one day.

Caribou live differently from the moose we saw earlier. In contrast to moose, which feed hidden in the trees, caribou graze out in the open, where they can easily see and outrun a wolf or a bear. Also, caribou are herd animals, while moose like living alone. A single moose can hide easily among the trees, but a herd of caribou can't. Isn't it amazing how animals know all that? It's called 'instinct.'

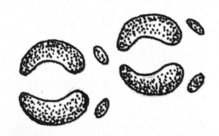

ALPINE ARNICA
PINK PLUME
ARCTIC GROUND SQUIRREL

Did you notice the little white specks high up on the hillside in the previous picture? Did you miss them or did you think they were patches of snow? The driver points out that those are animals. Can you believe it? He must have eagle eyes. Fortunately, we brought a pair of binoculars. Otherwise we would have missed seeing these beautiful Dall sheep up close.

"Dall sheep spend most of their time high up on hillsides and rugged mountain slopes where they are safe from their main predators, bears and wolves," the driver explains.

He has already talked much about bears and wolves, hasn't he? Even without having seen any yet, their presence is certainly noticeable in the behavior of other animals. That, too, is a sign that everything is part of one big ecosystem. Even things you don't see right away can affect other creatures' behavior.

What a coincidence! Just as the driver mentions wolves and just as the bus passes the Teklanika River, here's a wolf crossing the river at the exact same time. And what a beautiful wolf it is!

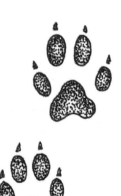

We really didn't expect to see a wolf because only between 150 to 200 of them live in the park. "Actually," the driver says, "chances to see a wolf on this trip are very good right now. There's a wolf den in this valley we are currently driving through and, occasionally, we even see some wolf pups! Also, wolves normally live and hunt in packs. So keep looking. We may see another one nearby."

DWARF FIREWEED

NORTHERN RED-BACKED VOLE

Have you ever heard wolves howling at the moon at night? Some people on the bus stayed at this campground and are telling now that they heard two wolf packs howling at each other last night. Don't you get goose bumps just hearing about it?

There are several campgrounds for tent and RV campers in the park, and the backcountry is wide open for everyone with the courage to brave the wild. Camping among wild animals isn't everybody's cup of tea. How about you? Would you dare to sleep in a tent knowing that wolves and other wild animals might be nearby and watching you?

WHITE SPRUCE

GRAY JAY

BOREAL CHICKADEE

Oh, oh, look out! There's danger ahead! This sign warns visitors not to leave the road for the next 5 miles. We wonder why?

"Why shouldn't we leave the road here and what's the deal with the nails in the sign?" someone asks the driver. He responds, "This area is closed to off-road travel because it is prime bear country. And the nails were put into this sign by the park service. Before there were any nails, bears would scratch their backs so hard on the sign that it would fall over. Actually, it's a problem all over the park."

Between 250 and 300 bears live in the park and it is this area, known as Sable Pass, where there is the best chance to see one. Let's get our cameras ready.

LONG-TAILED JAEGER

BEAR FLOWER

Everybody on the bus hoped to see one or two bears, but nobody was prepared for this. Four bears together and so close to the bus! What a magnificent sight! And how cute the two little cubs are playing. But Mama bear doesn't look very friendly, does she?

"I want to take a close-up picture! Open the door!" one of the passengers requests.
"Oh no," the driver responds. "For one, I'm not allowed to let anybody out. Second, you'd be rather crazy to get so close to a bear. Normally, bears have a natural fear of people and usually run away when they hear or smell a human. However, when a bear has young cubs like this one or when a hiker happens to surprise her, she may charge to defend herself, her cubs, or their food. Nobody gets off here!"

BLACK-BILLED MAGPIE

SHORT-TAILED WEASEL

The bus driver may think that it would be crazy to get off the bus here, but people lived in this area among the grizzly bears long before it was made a national park.

In the very early days, Athabaskan Indians lived and hunted here during the summer months. Shortly after the United States purchased Alaska from Russia in 1867, adventurers and explorers started heading north to Alaska to strike it rich looking for gold. The first ones arrived in this area a little more than 100 years ago. This picture from a guide book shows an old log cabin that may have been built by one of them. Among the adventurers was a gentleman named Charles Sheldon, who fell so much in love with this wilderness area that he lobbied the United States government to declare this land an animal refuge. Fortunately, he succeeded in 1917 with the creation of Mt. McKinley National Park. In 1980, the government increased the park's size and renamed it Denali National Park and Preserve.

A historic cabin in Denali National Park and Preserve once sheltered the early pioneers exploring this area. Many of these buildings are in use today. They provide shelter for people conducting winter research. It might be fun to imagine what it was like to live in

SANDHILL CRANES

BOG BLUEBERRY

LOW-BUSH CRANBERRY

BROWN LEMMING

MOSSBERRY

ALPINE BEARBERRY

Can you imagine living here all year long in a small log cabin and among all the wild animals? We are here in the summer when it is nice and warm, but how is it during the rest of the year?

Luckily, the guide book is full of neat pictures. Just look at these gorgeous fall colors! And how about all those caribou! It says in the book that large herds of caribou migrate in the fall from summer grazing areas in the east to wintering grounds in the western part of the park. Wouldn't it be great to see a caribou migration one day?

Oh look, there's another ptarmigan in the picture! It has started growing white feathers. You know what that means, don't you? It means that winter is near.

WILLOW PTARMIGAN IN FALL

AUTUMN LANDSCAPE IN THE PARK

AS THE TEMPERATURES BECOME COOLER
APPROACH OF AUTUMN, THE FOLI
ANGE COLORS. BEAUTIF

COMMON RAVEN

The guide book also shows a winter scene. Hmm, that's strange. Isn't it supposed to be all dark in Alaska during the winter?

"Oh no," the driver responds. "We are too far south for that. You have to be much further north to experience continuous darkness during the winter. Here at the park, even on December 21st, the shortest day of the year, we have a good 4 and 1/2 hours of daylight."

Okay, but what's the deal with the dog sled? Surely nobody still uses dog sleds anymore in this age of snowmobiles!

"Wrong again," the driver explains. "Quite a few Alaskans still use dog sleds, mostly as a hobby or for sport. Here in the park, where the road is closed to motorized vehicles during the winter, dogs and sleds are used by the Park Service to patrol the back country."

WOLVERINE

ERMINE (WEASEL IN WINTER COAT)

A DOGTEAM ON PATROL

Oh, oh, we better put the guide book away or we might miss something!

"This area is known as Polychrome Pass," the driver announces. "Polychrome means 'many colors.' These colorful rocks are volcanic and are millions of years old. We are almost 700 feet above the valley bottom. There will be a 15-minute rest stop at the top of the pass."

What a thrill to ride a bus along a steep mountain-side! The view is spectacular! And look how little the big river looks from way up here. Going around the curves is like being on a roller coaster. It's good that we aren't afraid of heights. How about you? Are you afraid of heights?

GOLDEN EAGLE WITH CHICKS

Speaking of heights, one of the highlights of this trip into the park is to see North America's highest mountain, Mt. McKinley. It is also known under its Native Alaskan name, Denali, meaning the 'Great One.' From here we should have a fantastic view of this spectacular mountain.

"Where is it, where is it?" everybody asks. "Well," the driver answers, "you should know that only about 1 in 3 visitors actually sees Mt. McKinley. Even on a beautiful day, like today, it can be hidden behind clouds, because a massive mountain like this one can create its own weather system. But if you look straight ahead, you can see Denali peeking out at the very top of the clouds." Seeing many disappointed faces, he finally adds, "Now listen up, everybody. Don't be upset. There's still a chance to see Denali from farther down the road."

ARCTIC TERNS

RED FOX FAMILY

ARCTIC POPPY

Oh boy, was he right or what? The bus arrived at the end of the route, at a place called Wonder Lake, and the clouds have totally disappeared. The entire mountain is right in front of us - all of its 20,320 feet.

Can you imagine climbing Mt. McKinley? More than one thousand climbers try it each year, but only about half of them make it to the top. It's a tough mountain to climb because, as you can see, it's winter up there all year long. Temperatures can go down to minus 90 degrees Fahrenheit and winds can blow at 150 mph on the mountain. That's too rough for most! How about you? Would you like to climb Denali one day?

BEAVER

COMMON LOON

It's getting late now, as signaled by the setting sun creating a spectacular display of pink colors, called alpenglow, on the mountains of the Alaska Range.

We head back to our hotel rooms after a great day, feeling good about the fact that nature still can do her own thing here at Denali National Park and Preserve, with little impact from people. The National Park Service certainly does a good job making sure of that. Their work will ensure that this park will remain a wild place for many generations of visitors to come. We hope you will be one of them one day and that you will enjoy it as much as we did today.

This is **THE END**

of another great adventure at Denali National Park.

PORCUPINE

GRAY WOLVES

Your Photos Here

Your Travel Log Here

_____

_____

_____

_____

_____

_____

_____

_____

_____

_____

_____

_____

Your Photos Here

Your Travel Log Here

_____

_____

_____

_____

_____

_____

_____

_____

_____

_____

_____

_____

Your Photos Here

Your Travel Log Here

More Children's Books by Bernd and Susan Richter

Saddle Pal Creations, P.O. Box 872127, Wasilla, AK 99687; www.alaskachildrensbooks.com

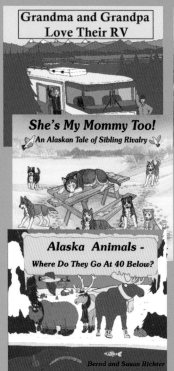

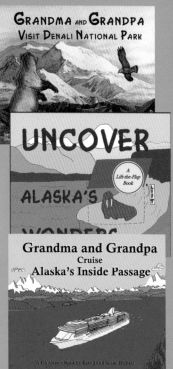

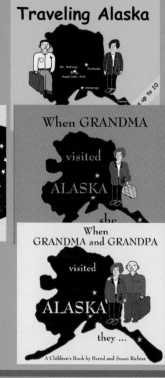

Old Maid - card game

Board Books

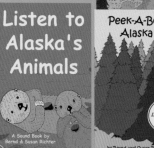

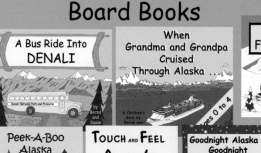